Drac, tell us about

modernism

H KLICZKOWSKI

Drac, tell us about

modernism

Edgardo Minond and Miguel Minond

Dedicated to my niece Julia Di Veroli Silberberg
H. A. K

HK Concept and idea: Hugo Kliczkowski and Paco Asensio

Coordinating editor: Aurora Cuito

Text: Meritxell Fernández

Drawings: Edgardo Minond and Miguel Minond

Translation: Books Factory *Translations*

Art Director: Mireia Casanovas Soley

Graphic designer and layout: Emma Termes Parera

Photographers: Marc Mormeneo: 8, 9, 14, 44, 45, 47, 62
Pere Planells: 10, 11, 15, 16, 28
Miquel Tres: 34, 35, 36, 37, 40, 41, 42, 48, 49, 50,
58, 60, 61, 63, 64, 65, 67, 68, 69, 72 (bottom),
73, 74, 75
Joana Furió: 26, 32
Melba Levick: 20, 21, 24, 53, 54, 55, 72 (left and right)
Az Disseny S.L.: 70, 71

Copyright for the international edition
© H Kliczkowski-Onlybook, S.L.
La Fundición, 15. Polígono Industrial Santa Ana
28529 Rivas-Vaciamadrid. Madrid
Tel.: +34 91 666 50 01
Fax: +34 91 301 26 83
onlybook@asppan.com
www.onlybook.com

Editorial project

LOFT Publications
Via Laietana, 32 4º Of. 92
08003 Barcelona. Spain
Tel.: +34 932 688 088
Fax: +34 932 687 073
e-mail: loft@loftpublications.com
www.loftpublications.com

Printed by:
Anman Gràfiques del Vallès,
Spain

March 2003

ISBN: 84-96137-13-9
DL: B-01733-03

Visit Modernist buildings with your new friends

Nabil

Li

Eric

Fina

Park Güell

It is a lovely sunny Sunday and Li, Fina, Nabil and Eric have gone for a walk with their parents. After a sumptuous breakfast the adults are engaged in lively conversation. Nearby, the children, looking a little bit bored, are sitting on a bench, looking around and waiting for something exciting to happen.

"Why don't we have a race?" Nabil asks the others.
"Great idea!" they all shout out in agreement.
"OK! Ready, set, go!!!"

"Uh! How boring!"

The children dash off and race down the stairs to the bottom.

"I won!" Eric shouts.

"No way! I've been here for a long time," a friendly voice says. The kids look at each other and then notice that the dragon of Gaudí is standing next to them.

"Good morning! My name is Drac."

"How strange, a talking dragon…!!

"Of course I can speak and I'd like to propose that we go for a walk around the park. As you have all probably already noticed, to enter into this park is to enter into a world of magic. And one of the reasons is the modernist elements here. I've been a part of modernism for a long time and I can explain a lot of things to you about modernism. What do you all think? Would you like me to do that?"

"A splendid idea! Count me in. And you guys?" Eric asks them.

"I wouldn't miss it for anything in the world."

"Come on then! Let's go!"

"This is the column space. It is under the square where the curvy benches are, remember, where you began racing from. Gaudí came up with a drainage system for when it rained. How do do you think the water is drained away?"

"I don't see any drain pipes or gutters," Fina answered.

"If you'll notice on the ceiling, you'll see that it is a little bit slanted at every column, and this is where the water flows and then it comes out through my mouth. It's an ingenious solution, isn't it. It was Gaudí's idea. He was the architect who built this park and one of the greatest exponents of modernism. He had many followers and one of them, Jujol, designed the large ceramic medallions that you can see on the ceiling."

"Wow!" they all exclaim as they raise their heads.

"How big!"

"These columns are not as straight as the ones in the column space. Why is that?" Fina asks.

"They can't be straight because they have to adapt to the slope of the bald mountain, which was the name for this place. When the Count Eusebi Güell commissioned Gaudí with the construction of this park, his idea was to build a city in the middle of a garden, like the ones he had seen abroad. That's why he had to adapt the lots to the natural features of the terrain. Fortunately, only two lots were sold. So, in 1923 it was taken over by the city and they decided to make it into a public park where people could come and stroll."

Suddenly, Drac disappears. Can you see him? Imagine that it's a magic dragon and can change colors.

"Hey, dragon. Please, don't leave yet. You could explain some more things about modernism to us, OK?"

"Ha ha ha. Let's see if you can find me!"

"Well, if you'd like to see more modernist buildings, then we could head off to the Sagrada Família," Drac says as he comes out of his hiding place.

They leave Park Güell and head for Sagrada Família.

Sagrada Família

"Francisco Paula de Villar began the construction of it more than a hundred years ago. A short time after he started, Gaudí took over for him. This is the Nativity façade. It's like a gigantic nativity scene. Do you see what I mean?"

"It's very, very beautiful!"

This complex was to incorporate various schools and workshops for the workers of the neighborhood, out of which only one children's school was built. We can't see the whole thing from here, let's go higher!

The five of them are going up the great winding staircase to get to the top of the tower. Drac continues explaining things to them.

"When the church is finished, it will have twelve towers, one for each of the twelve apostles, and one very tall one in the middle that will soar up to 170 meters, which will represent Jesus Christ."

"When it's finished, will we be able to go up to the top?" Eric asks.

"Naturally, but there is still a lot of work to do."

"So, we'll be grown up by then?"

"Yes, but don't worry. There's a very good chance that you kids will see it finished, unlike Gaudí, who died before. You see, he was run over by a tram right here in front. He was taken to the Hospital de la Santa Creu and because he wasn't carrying any identification, they thought he was a tramp. Poor Gaudí! He was so absorbed in his work at Sagrada Família that he had left his briefcase at home. And speaking of hospitals, would you like to visit a modernist hospital?"

"OK."

They say goodbye to Sagrada Família and head off to Hospital de Sant Pau.

Hospital de Sant Pau

Once at the hospital, Drac suggests that they have lunch. The walk has given them an appetite. They sit down on the grass and while they eat, he continues with his explanations.

"This hospital was built by Domènech i Montaner. Notice the decoration of the buildings. It represents the history of Catalonia and is mixed with floral motifs and animals."

"It looks like a small city!" Li says.

"His original plan was to build a city in the middle of a garden, like Park Güell."

'Mmm, it's so tasty.'

19

"Modernist architects often designed in stained glass windows. When we visit the Palau de la Música, we'll also get to see some like these."

From here we can see some of the wards. There are 48 altogether and they are con-
nected by underground passageways. Nevertheless, soon it will no longer be a hospital as in the future, they want it to be converted exclusively into a landmark and tou-
rist attraction. A tour bus will take you around for a short tour in the interior of the
complex, and then take you down to the Sagrada Família, just the opposite route that
we've taken today. In fact, this bus is already in service and some Barcelona children
have already made the visit."

"It occurred to me that maybe I could propose to my teacher at school, that our class
take this tour," Nabil mentioned. "In my class their are children from different parts
of the world and I'm sure that some of them have never seen these monuments before," he finished.

They leave Hospital de Sant Pau behind and head for Casa Terrades.

Casa Terrades

The five friends arrive to Casa Terrades on wheels.
On arriving, they gaze upon it in awe.

"Wow! It looks like an enchanted castle. How
beautiful it would be if it were alone on top of a
mountain!" Fina exclaims with emotion.

"You're not far from the truth. In fact, although
now it is surrounded by buildings, when it was
constructed, it was standing alone."

"This building is also known as the Casa de las Punxes (needles), because of the shape that the building has. Based on three houses and getting his inspiration from medieval castles, Josep Puig i Cadafalch remodeled it. He made use of very modernist elements such as wrought iron, glazed ceramics and the figure of Sant Jordi, who is the patron saint of Catalonia."

"On Sant Jordi's Day my father gave me a red rose as a present," Fina said.

"And my father gave me a very entertaining book of adventures!"

"This tradition has even made its way to Japan. On April twenty-third people give books and roses to each other as presents, and everybody goes out for a stroll in the streets!" Li explains.

They leave Casa Terrades behind and are off to Casa Milà.

Casa Milà, la Pedrera

Drac and his friends walk down Passeig de Gràcia until they come to Casa Milà.

"The Milà-Segimon Family commissioned Gaudí with the construction of it. Look closely. It looks like an enormous rocky mountain and that is why the people called it the Pedrera (stonequarry). Look at the façade and at the curvy, undulating surface. Doesn't it remind you of the waves of the sea?"

"You're right! The ground floor looks like the entrance to an underwater grotto in the sea," Li exclaims with surprise.

"And those strange-looking balconies?"

"They are made of wrought iron and are in the shape of flowers and leaves."

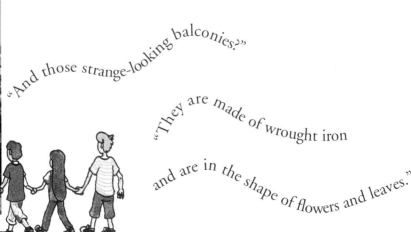

The children follow Drac into the building.

"The headquarters for the Fundació Caixa Catalunya are here. They are in charge of the restoration and pre-servation of some of Gaudí's works. I've got a great idea! Why don't we all lie down on the floor and then we can admire the ceiling. Come on!"

Those clouds are so big!

Thrilled with the idea, the children let themselves plop down noisily onto the floor.

"How fun!" Nabil cries. "Our parents would never let us do this!"

"The ceiling also looks like the ocean, with waves, sand, beach…"

"But, over there, I see flowers!" Eric retorts.

"And I see a cloud in the middle of the sky!"

"If you'd like to see the sky, then let's go up to the roof. There, we can see the chimneys."

"Wow! What flowers!"

"The chimneys are adorned with Gaudí's famous 'trencadís', like my skin!" Drac explained laughing. "Some are covered with small pieces of ceramic and others with pieces of bottles. Would you all like to adorn one?"
"Yeah!!!" they all responded together.

Yellow!!

Blue!!

Red!!

Drac moves his hands up and down and takes out some boxes full of small, colored ceramic pieces. Then, they decorate the chimneys.

"How pretty it looks. When I get home, I'll cut colored construction paper into little pieces and decorate a box for mother, 'trencat' Gaudí style," Li explains.

"'Trencadís' style" Eric corrects, as he smiles at the little one.

Nabil leaves the group to reconnoiser the area. Suddenly, he comes back running and shouting:

"I've seen some soldiers!"

"Where? Can we go to see them, Drac?"

"Of course. Let's go have a look at those soldiers."

"They're gigantic!" Fina exclaims.

"These chimneys have different shapes. They're so big that you can see them all the way from the street. Did you notice before? Look, over there! There are four soldiers that look a lot like you. Stand together next to them and I'll take photograph so you can give it to your parents. Li can keep it inside her Gaudí box. Or, you can even frame it!"

"Cheeeese!!"

They leave casa Milà and head for the Editorial Montaner i Simón.

Editorial Montaner i Simón

"Before constructing Hospital de Sant Pau, Domènech i Montaner built this building. That's why they look so similar. The difference is that this was built for industrial uses, specifically to set up a large printing factory, the Editorial Montaner i Simón. At the present, it houses the Fundació Tàpies and a very large specialized library."

"Where is Li?" Fina asks. Drac and the children search for Li all throughout the library. Since they can't shout, they have to look in all of the aisles. At the last bookcase they find her. She is looking at some books and it's obvious, that she is very fascinated.

"They are all art books and books on Asian culture!" she says.

"Come on kids! Let's go visit the Museu Tàpies. There are some hammocks there!"

They all jump and laugh on top of the hammock until…

"Plop, everybody to the floor!!"

"Look, kids. Tàpies does not only make sculptures. He also paints. Look at those paintings. Do you like them?"

"Yeeeees!" they all responded.

"Whopssss, Nabil! If he doesn't tie his shoes, he's certainly going to become a good Tàpies!" Li laughs.

Drac takes them up to the roof to admire a very famous Tàpies sculpture.

"It looks like a cloud!" Fina observes.

"Well, yes, in fact. It's named *Núvol i cadira* and it represents a cloud and a chair. Are you getting hungry?"

"I'm starving," Nabil says. "You wouldn't happen to have any candy, would you?"

"I've got something better in mind. I know a pastry shop that's so good that it makes your mouth water."

They leave Editorial Montaner i Simón behind and head for Casa Figueres.

39

casa Figueres

On entering the Pastisseria Escribà in Casa Figueres, Nabil is awe-struck when he sees the boxes of chocolates in the shop window. The boxes are of modernist style.

"Let's see. What would you like?" Drac asks as he dons a baker's hat.

The children ask him for pastries, chocolates, cookies…

"Mummmmm, everything is just delicious!"

"Come on Drac. I'll be the waiter now while you tell us things about this shop," Eric says, as he imagines himself dressed up in waiter's clothes.

"Years ago, this was a grocery store where they used to sell a little bit of everything. At the beginning of the twentieth century, many merchants liked the modernist style and they thought it was useful for attracting the bourgeoisie into their shops. In this shop you can find the work of different artists and artisans from around the city. We can admire the magnificent mosaics, the stained glass windows, the relief sculptures, and the letters on the sign, which are all of traditional modernist style."

"Sir, your pastry," Eric offers. He seems to have seriously taken up the role of waiter.

"Mummmm! And now, I'm going to eat this pastry! When we finish, I'll take you all to another lovely place."

They leave Casa Figueres and head for Plaça Reial.

Lamppost in Plaça Reial

"Well, here we are. This is Plaça Reial. The city hall commissioned Gaudí with the task of designing these three streetlights next to the *Tres Gràcies* fountain. They are teeming with modernists symbols such as flowers, mythological animals and the coat of arms of the city. When they were last restored, they were painted with bright colors which not everyone liked."

"Look closely and you'll see that nowadays the streetlights are electric. Before, however, they used gas like in your kitchens. Have you ever noticed how your mother lights the range? Look! It would be more or less like this…"

Drac takes a flame from his mouth and lights one of the streetlights.

"There used to be men whose job was light all of the streetlights in the city."

"Yes, they were the night watchmen. My grandfather told me once that it was their job also to open and close the main door of the houses and residential buildings for the people," Fina pointed out.

"If you want to get a better view, we could go up on the roof of one of these houses. At night, this place is bustling with people who come to listen to music, chat, dance…"
Drac grabs a child with each of his feet and flies up to the roof.
"One day we came here with our parents and we were dancing down there below. Do you remember, Fina? You came, too," Nabil said.
"That's right. We must have looked so small from up here!"

46

"Imagine all of the Rambla lined with these streetlights. The town hall decided that all of the main streets should have streetlights by different designers. It would have been beautiful, don't you think? It's a pity that the project wasn't carried out."

They leave Plaça Reial behind and head for the Museu de Zoologia.

Museu de zoología

Hey, Drac, they're like you!!

"Now, we are inside of the Parc de la Ciutadella. Domènech i Montaner desig-
ed this building here that is called the Castell dels Tres Dracs (castle of the three
ragons). This is thanks to its appearance and to my little cousins here," Drac
xplains as he enthusiastically greets the small reptiles on the outside.

It looks like the Castle of Camelot, you know, the one in the tale about Merlin
ne wizard!"

This building has housed many different things. First, it was a café and shortly
hereafter, it was an artisans workshop where you could learn things such as 'tren-
adís'. Later, it was a history museum, a music school, a biology museum… And
astly, it has now been converted into the Museu de Zoologia.

ou can have a gui-
ed tour or you can
isit it on your own.
They also offer cour-
es, workshops, exhi-
bitions, and studies
on the wildlife of
Catalonia."

"When I grow up, I
vant to work here,
vith the animals,"
Fina says.

Once inside the museum, the children are left speechless while they watch films with lions and other wild animals in them. Suddenly, Drac realizes that Fina is missing. He is worried since she went off without saying anything to the others. Finally, he finds her. She's enthusiastically observing what's inside a glass display cabinet.

"There are tons of birds here." As they finish the visit at the museum, Drac has a new proposal for them.

"Would you like to listen to some music?"

"I love music," Eric replies.

"Well then, let's go!"

They leave the Museu de zoologia and head for the Palau de la Música.

51

Palau de la Música

"The Palau de la Música is anothe
building by Domènech i Montaner. H
was commissioned to build it by th
Orfeó Català. This is an institution fo
the promotion of popular Catalar
music, created by Lluís Millet."

Roooosa d'abriiiiiil…

"Look at this magnificent hall! The dome, the ceiling, the arches… Everything is beautifully designed for listening to music."

Drac entones a song and the children applaud and laugh with delight.

"What are those statues way up there?" Fina asks.

"Those are the Muses. Come on, everybody, come here!" Drac shouts as he places th
two girls on the statues.

"Wow! What beautiful Muses!" Eric comments laughingly.

"The Muses are the goddesses of the arts and sciences: music, writing, architecture..
They give the creators the inspiration to make their works. Even so, the creators hav
to work hard if they want to be able to offer us works of beauty."

"Thanks to those large windows and the dome, a lot of sunlight comes in here."

"And at night?" Nabil asks.

"Well of course, there's no other choice but to turn on the lamps."

"Hey, Drac! Don't leave just yet! There's something else that we have to tell these children," a voice says to them.

One of the figures from the group of statues on the façade of the Palau, has come alive. It's climbing down. Now, it comes up to the kids.

"We have to remember that music is very important. When you are sad, or happy, or when you are with your parents on the beach, you like to listen to it, don't you? We should try to get everyone to love and respect it, and this includes everything related to it. We are tired of being painted, or having things thrown at us that make the walls dirty."

"Thanks comrade. I'm sure that we can count on them to help us out."

"Isn't that right, kids?" Drac asks.

"Yeeees!"

"Bye, see you next time"

They leave the Palau de la Música and head off to the Monumental.

Plaça de Toros Monumental

"Well, here we are! This modernist construction was built by two fine architects, Ignasi Mas and Domènech Sugrañes, at the end of the modernist period. As you can see, though they only used two colors for the ceramics, they elaborated very distinct shapes and drawings. Flowers, stars, waves and words, decorate the outside walls, and as we'll see later, also the inside ones."

"I can see the Sagrada Família from here!" Li blurts out.

"And down there, you can see the Torre Mapfre and the Hotel Arts!"

"Boy! How wide this street is! We'll have to be careful crossing it, won't we?" Fina points out.

"Yes. Nabil, can you take her hand?" Drac asks him.

"These are the ticket windows. This is where we buy the tickets. How many of us are there? One, two, three, four… and one for me!"

Each child takes a ticket and they go into the bullring.

"Nowadays, they use this bullring for many diverse things. All different types of concerts are held here. On some occasions, they even set up a circus with clowns, trapeze artists, acrobats, tigers, horses… It's great fun!"

"Come on! Let's go inside."

They leave the Monumental and head for the Fàbrica Casaramona.

Fàbrica Casaramona

"This factory exemplifies, once again, how modernism spread to all areas in society. Before, we saw how industry supported the modernist movement. Do you remember the Fundació Tàpies?"

"It was a printing factory, wasn't it?"

"That's right. This building was designed by Josep Puig i Cadafalch. It was a textile factory where they made all types of fabrics and similar things for clothes. Not long ago, it was bought by the Fundació La Caixa and was given the name of Caixa Fòrum. It is a cultural and art center where painting and photography exhibitions are held, and where you can see documentaries and films."

"Can we go up on the terrace?"

"Yes, but be careful because it's very high."

"From up on the terrace we can see the Palau Nacional de Montjuïc, the Magic Fountain, and Eixample and Poble Sec quarters."

"Look! I can see our house over there!" Eric shouts as he points at a building far away.

"Can you see it, children?"

"How cool!"

"Have you noticed? This roof is very large," Nabil says.

"I'd like to play something. What could we play?" Eric asks.

"I say, let's play hide-and-seek," Fina suggests.

"I'd prefer to play tag," Li answers as she starts chasing after Fina.

"OK kids, don't start fighting! I've got another idea. We can play a guessing game. We can try to guess what the different towers are made of."

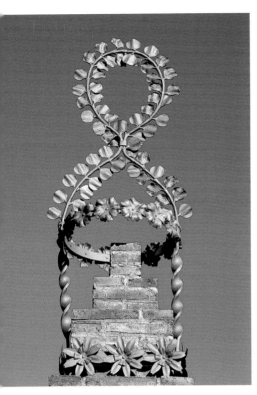

There's a flower-shaped one made of wrought iron."

The ceramic one has drawings."

And the square one is made of bricks."

And with the letters: C, A, S, A, R, A, M, O, N, A."

Casa Casaramona!!"

Very good, children. Little by little we have learned a little bit more about modernism, and all of the things it made use of. Now, we had better get back to Park Güell, before it gets dark. Let's go!"

They leave fábrica Casaramona and head for park Güell

The children and Drac meet again in front of Park Güell.

"It's been an absolutely fabulous tour!"

"Yes, and we have learned a lot of new things about modernism," Eric said.

"And we've made a new friend, a very special new friend!" Fina says as she gives Dra a big hearty hug.

"Oh, and now, are you going to stay here? Why don't you come along with us?"

"I'd love to Li, but I'm afraid that I can't. I have to stay here on the steps. This way when other kids come along, I can take them on a tour just like I did with all of you But from now on, you know where I am and what my name is. So, all you have t do is call out my name loudly, and I'll be at your side in a snap. Besides, you ca come and visit me here in the park anytime you want. You've been great little eage students!! See you all real soon! Bye-bye!!!"

Once again, Drac becomes immobile at his place on the steps in the park. The children go greet their parents and excitedly explain everything that they've been doing.

"Bye-bye my friends!! See you soon!!"

Modernist
features

stained
glass
windows

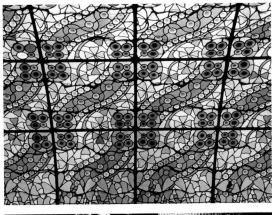

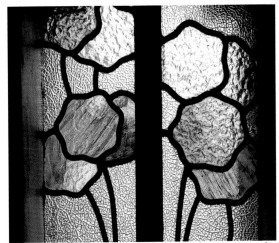

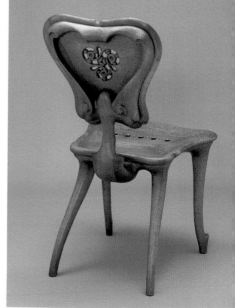

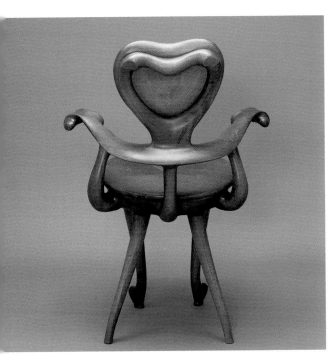

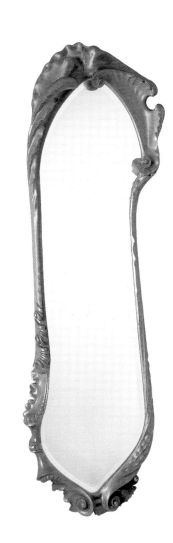

Furniture

Mosaics

sculptures

aça de les
òries

Visit Modernism

1. **Park Güell**
   Olot, s/n

2. **Sagrada Família**
   Plaça de la Sagrada Família

3. **Hospital de Sant Pau**
   Sant Antoni Maria Claret, 167

4. **Casa Terrades**
   Diagonal, 416

5. **Casa Milà**
   Passeig de Gràcia, 92

6. **Fundació Tàpies**
   Aragó, 255

7. **Casa Figueres**
   Rambla Caputxins, 83

8. **Lampposts by Plaça Reial**
   Plaça Reial

9. **Museu de Zoologia**
   Parc de la Ciutadella

10. **Palau de la Música**
    Sant Pere Més Alt, 13

11. **Monumental**
    Gran via de les corts Catalanes, 747

12. **Fàbrica Casaramona**
    Marqués de Comillas, 6-8

other modernist places that you can visit

Others titles from this collection

La Fundición, 15 Polígono Industrial Santa Ana 28529 Rivas-Vaciamadrid Madrid Tel. 34 91 666 50 01 Fax 34 91 301 26 83 asppan@asppan.com www.onlybook.com

Barcelona, explica'ns Gaudí/Barcelona, cuéntanos de Gaudí/Barcelona, tell us about Gaudí
ISBN: (C)   84-89439-32-X
ISBN: (E)   84-89439-29-X
ISBN: (GB) 84-89439-28-1

Barcelona, parla'ns de tu/Barcelona, cuéntanos de ti/Barcelona, tell us about yourself
ISBN: (C)   84-96048-34-9
ISBN: (E)   84-96048-33-0
ISBN: (GB) 84-96048-36-5

Madrid, cuéntanos de ti/Madrid, tell us about yourself
SBN: (E)   84-96048-99-3
ISBN: (GB) 84-96137-56-2

Drac, explica'ns el Modernisme/Drac, cuéntanos del Modernismo/Drac, tell us about Modernism
ISBN: (C)   84-96137-12-0
ISBN: (E)   84-96137-11-2
ISBN: (GB) 84-96137-13-9